Passion
and
Pain

Passion

and

Pain

Prose, Poems,
Psalms, and Proverbs

Stephen E. Hooks

iUniverse, Inc.
Bloomington

Passion and Pain
Prose, Poems, Psalms, and Proverbs

iUniverse books may be ordered through booksellers or by contacting:

iUniverse
1663 Liberty Drive
Bloomington, IN 47403
www.iuniverse.com
1-800-Authors (1-800-288-4677)

ISBN: 978-1-4502-9455-3 (sc)
ISBN: 978-1-4502-9457-7 (hc)
ISBN: 978-1-4502-9456-0 (ebk)

Printed in the United States of America

iUniverse rev. date: 06/27/2012

Contents

Introduction..ix

Prose 1

Poems..47

Psalms/Proverbs..119

Acknowledgement...133

Photo Credits 135

To my mother Deborah Ficklin who loves me unconditionally. Thank you! Your Passion for GIVING to humanity is Inspiring.

To Steven J. Hooks, Thank You!
Your Pain in LIVING is my Motivation.

To the people who have been a part of my evolution, you have been my muse. Thank You!

Introduction

Age of VIRGO: The Virgin
Stephen E. Hooks 09-11-1974

Your realm is a place of order, serenity, and refinement. You have a literary flair, a practical mind, and love of detail. Your considerate nature is a sanctuary for your friends, but in love you seek true feelings, and would rather be alone than be taken casually. Your attention to detail can go overboard, but your lack of compromise assures perfect results. August 24-September 23

My writing comes from the depth of my spirit translated by my soul. It is important that I share my heart and mind in hopes it may trigger a spark in another young male to become free, as I have discovered writing is liberating for the soul of a man. My intentions for writing this book are to offer consolation and inspiration to anyone who can relate. My motivation for the composition of this book is my Dad Steven James Hooks. He has written me many times from his prison cell to offer me understanding of himself, I met my dad through his writings in prison. While in prison my dad was sober free from drugs and alcohol, I believe his times in prison were his salvation periods, in prison he released his passion and pain on paper and mailed it to me.

There are many males like me who grew up with their father absent from home, and the pain of that void was numbing to our souls. We suffer from the disconnectedness of our relationship with our fathers and some of us never find the remedy for our salvation. I began writing consistently after receiving letters from my dad while he was in prison and I was on a spiritual journey to find knowledge of God and Self. Over a period of fifteen years I composed the writings in this book. My writing is fused with passion from beautiful relationships I've experienced with my mother, grandmother, friends, and the wonders of creation. My writing is constructed with the pain I've experienced through loss, guilt, shame, fear, and bad decisions.

The theme of this book is my father and I share a unique bond without a consistent communal relationship. Our relationship was initiated through words on paper, which gave me a resolution and helped me identify the subliminal gift I received from him. Through his writings I understood his pain, as a 9-year-old boy losing his mother and his father, also a drug addict bound by his internal pain of an estranged relationship with his father. I took my dad's pain mixed with my pain and added our passion for writing and created this book.

This book is about the power of words, how a son found his dad through letters from prison, but also his voice and the ability to find himself through his own writing. I hope the writings from this book generate a movement for writing for the sake of healing the souls of males in urban communities and prisons. Many of us men are congested with anger, bitterness, regret, doubt, fear, and other misdiagnosed dis-eases. Imagine if we started a revolution for writing in the early stages of development in our urban communities, giving a young male a safe outlet for his misunderstood emotions, we might decrease the prison population. I hope my book finds its intended reader and provides hope and consolation.

These writings are from my journey thus far. I use prose poetry and psalmic proverbs, which allow me to be free, not worried about traditional form but liberal for self-expression. I wrote for many years with a vulnerable heart during some distraught periods of my life. During the time of composing this book I channeled inspiration from two of the greatest poets of my generation, TUPAC SHAKUR and JILL SCOTT. I listened to the CD and read the

poems from Tupac's work THE ROSE T CONCRETE. Tupac's art, coming fron gave me the confidence to write from a p revealing my serious demeanor as a man. I music; in her art I conceived the feminine gave me the confidence to reveal my sensi

The Harlem Renaissance has influenc era are celestial. I am reminded of auth Baldwin, Paul Lawrence Dunbar, James V Wright, and Alex Hailey, they left a legacy generation.

"There is no better way to get inside the mind and heart of an artist than to examine his Artistic Expression."

> Leila Steinberg
> Former Manager of Tupac Amaru Shakur
> Excerpt from the book "The Rose that grew from the concrete."

"A man should conceive of a legitimate purpose in his heart, and set out to accomplish it."

> James Allen

Prose

Written or spoken language in its ordinary form, without metrical
   structure
—Figurative plain or dull writing, discourse, or expression

Prose Poetry

A piece of writing in prose, having obvious poetic qualities, including
   intensity, compactness, prominent rhythms, and imagery.

Psalm

A sacred song or hymn expressed in Worship

Proverb

A short pithy saying in general use, stating a general truth or piece
   of advice

Prose

Words I may never say . . .

As for the pain inside of you unseen by men, we've judged you merciless and unjust, without comprehension, ignorant of your experiences.

As gifted as you are only few know,

I know your soul through poetry.

In anger I threw those poems away you sent me from prison, I regarded them as bullshit words on a sheet of paper, not as the revelation of your soul, the part of you that is free and sober from drugs and alcohol. A moment of freedom from anguish of your vexed soul, a break from the torment of the demons that won't leave you alone, keeping you in bondage beyond physical chains, they subdued your soul from the moment you pierced the cervix of your mother.

I know your soul through poems.

A talented creation, ambushed, kidnapped, and molested by the evil, heartless streets, which enticed you. You lusted after the intoxicating HIGHS and LOWS of it's allure.

I empathize with your pain.

Who knows what they would have chosen if they were you?

Why, is the question I have?

I needed you there with me as a child, I wanted you there as an adolescent, I hated you as a young man, in my head I said "FUCK YOU!" so many times.

Many times, I wanted to fight you mano Y mano just to inflict bruises and pain on you as my soul bared from your absence.

Now I know that wouldn't have solved anything it would have only revealed outwardly your soul's inner essence. Beautiful as your eyes are, constantly disguised as evil, hazel brown surrounded by dark red.

I forgive you.

Aunt Peaches said you had a good heart as a boy you'd give the shirt off your back. Damn! Had you given me a shirt I'd frame it in gold and title it "My Inheritance"

Now, I am liberated! I am a Healed man, matured by LOVE, sustained by FAITH and anchored in HOPE.

I bless you.

I recognize you and why your journey took the course, it did.

I say to you.

I LOVE YOU DAD, the one whom God used for me to come into earth. I recognize the good and bad traits you passed to me.

I THANK YOU DAD, for my valuable inheritance. I've received a heart to dance, the gift of literature, and intelligence of a Hustler/ Harvard student.

As you did from your prison cells, I release my soul, and discover myself as I write on paper, words I may never say to you.

Man's Treasure

As a man embarking on the Manhood phase of my life, I've had to ask myself questions. The number one question being what do I value as a man? What is in my Treasure, my Treasure referring to my Heart (The core of my being, spirit/soul.) My master says good and evil comes from the Heart of Man and out of Man's spiritual resource and supply his mouth speaks. As for me, I've seen good and evil within myself. Now, I am aware of who I am, I plan to collect only appreciating jewels for my Treasure.

I admit until this chapter in my life I have treasured vanity. I have coveted money, success, expensive homes, clothes, and cars. I have treasured the external features of a woman more than the essence of her soul. I have created a self-image from various characters I've emulated. I confess my Treasure was full of perishable values and if you put fire and a strong wind to them, they'd vanish.

As I discover more truth on my journey through Manhood, I've had to determine what is profitable to keep in my Treasure. Is my acquisition of money, fame, and possessions what I want to remain in my Treasure at the end of my earth experience? When I'm deceased, what will my nephews say? What will my niece say about me? What will my family and friends say? On the day, they open up my Treasure, you know the day when everyone usually wears black. On the day, people, view a stuffed corpse laying supine in a decorated box. On that day, the Treasure will be unlocked, the scrolls read and the valuables of Heart revealed. What will be in my

Treasure? I hope I've discarded the evil and vanities of my soul and the remains are good, and when someone has a memory of me, they smile, as if stimulated by the flavor of a juicy watermelon on a hot summer day.

In a Man's Treasure (Heart) you will always find something, be it good or evil it's inevitable.

Thanks Ma!

Had you not prayed for me, I might be in an early grave,
Thanks for saying NO many times!
Had you been an alcohol consumer I might still be addicted to Malt
    Liquor,
Thanks for never drinking alcohol in my lifetime!
Had you allowed me to live without boundaries I'd have walked off
    a cliff and destroyed myself,
Thanks for teaching me accountability!
Had you gave me permission to have girlfriends as a boy I'd have a
    child prematurely,
Thanks for teaching me to preserve myself until marriage!
Had you released me to the streets I'd be in prison today,
Thanks for saying NO you can't hang with so & so.
Had you been a woman desperate for a man, I'd be an unhealthy man,
Thanks for being a loving devout single parent.
Had you been anyone other than the Woman you are,
I'd be a male destitute of my destiny of Manhood.
Thanks Ma, because of your prayers and faithfulness
I'VE BECOME A MAN!

Vanity, Vanity, Vanity, Meaningless, Meaningless, Meaningless

Money clothes a phat bankroll what type of life is that to live for?
Because in the end that don't mean shit!
When you appear before your maker it won't get you no respect.
Why we live to die, see but blind,
What do you live for? What will you die for?
We live without paying attention neglecting our souls
living lies chasing vanity.
I'm observing with my sixth sense
Yet, I too wanna have money like OPRAH,
I'm vain too.
I like Big Booties, Benzes, Beamers,
Struggle to be authentic,
I wish I were more simplistic.
Curious why we praise the bad neglect the good?
Maybe it's just me,
However, some things are vain and meaningless to me.

Simple Rule

If I learn this simple Rule
Everything else in life will be balanced
If I do what is right
I can overcome any of my challenges

If I obey this simple rule
I'll always have peace in my heart
If I follow the way that is good
I will begin my journey with a healthy start

If I perfect this simple rule
Others will delight in my presence
They will value what I say like a precious jewel
I speak of this simple rule.

Be honest.

Integrity

When I die let it be known
I strived to maintain my integrity
I remember the teacher asking
What matters to you?
I answered Character.

When I die let it be known
I failed many times but never quit
I lost some things but gained more
I hurt others but asked for forgiveness

When I die let it be said
He's genuine
He's unique
He was searching
He was lost
Yet in the end
He found

His Integrity.

Life or Death

"Is there anything in this world that you love
enough that U would kill for it or die for it?"
                              Bumpy Johnson "Hoodlum"

A son asks his father how much he loved him.
The Father said I love you so much I'd die for you.
The son replied Dad would you stop doing drugs, stop smoking,
    stop drinking?
Dad will you spend some time with me at home,
Dad will you come see me play basketball?
Dad I rather you not love me so much that you'd die for me
I'd rather you love me and Live with me.

Not until . . . .

I have experienced LOVE

I have discovered PEACE

I have known TRUTH

I have created WEALTH

I have evolved SPIRITUALLY

I have blessed EARTH

Will I contemplate DEATH

Not Until!

Mother's Day

When I was lonely
Too stubborn to call
You've been there.
When I was hurt
You put a bandage on me.
When I was tired
You prayed for my strength.
When I was in unnoticeable pain
You called, asking me how I felt.
You've been there when I hoped
It would be someone else,
Merciful, in spite my attitude
Modeling patience and love.
I know all that you give comes from God
You've always been there for me.
Thank You!
From your Son
Happy Mother's Day!

Encouraged by LOVE, Inspired by LOVE.

Hugs, kisses and the consistent words "I Love you."
Give strength to the weak,
Healing to the sick
If you knew, what love can do!
It's more than a feeling
More than a touch
An action born out of compassion
Oh, love! Does rebuild
Oh, love! Does restore
Oh, love! Does redeem
Once you've experienced love
You understand life

Between Saint and Sinner (unfinished)

Halleluiah!
The Hell with this!
                    My thoughts in a segment of time
Sometimes I feel like I live in two worlds
One I see with my natural eyes
                    Another within the sphere of my mind.
My heart too sensitive to be a macho man
I look into the future and see the young ones
                    My heart erupts with compassion,

Between Saint and Sinner

Mom has faith, maintains it today
All she ever does is pray, pray
A law-abiding citizen always trying to do what is right
She illuminates light.

Dad has faults, he maintains today
All he does is drink drink drink
A lawbreaker always in the justice system
He hides in the darkness.

Untitled

I wish he were there
I wish he told me he cared
I wish he had graduated from high school
I wish he didn't try so hard to be cool
I wish he could have been a provider
I wish he had stayed beside her
I wish he understood himself
I wish he knew
I wish he had accomplished his dreams
I wish he had never become a drug addict
I wish he could answer my Why's
I wish he heard my sisters cry
I wish he could start over again

If I had another wish

I'd wish I wasn't born of him
I'd wish he were successful
I'd wish he married a wife
I'd wish he raised his children
I'd wish he achieved his goals
I'd wish he lived righteous
I've wished this for my Dad,
All my life

What's Passion?

Is it a feeling? No! Passion for me is the essence of life beyond existing. Passion the substances deep inside me make me wanna die to live, suffocate to breathe, give my last to receive, vex my soul until it bleed. Passion my oasis is a desert when the journey is far its invisible fuel for my spirit as gas to my car. Passion, really it's hard for me to describe and give words to Passion beyond desire it will make a mountain move from its presence. Passion is so strong no emotion can compare. Passion uncontrolled is beyond ecstasy. Damn what can it be?

To me Passion can change the world at least in my perspective how I see.

Oh foolish me! How could I believe that anything such as this could possibly be?

Relationships

This is my hope for a RELATIONSHIP that enhances companionship and is the desire of other couples. Our RELATIONSHIP shouldn't be about money because money only solves money problems, our RELATIONSHIP shouldn't be based on appearance because someday we both will wrinkle and physically transform, our RELATIONSHIP shouldn't be about education because careers and jobs are uncertain, our RELATIONSHIP shouldn't be about status quo because our character is measured by what we value, our RELATIONSHIP shouldn't be about sex because minutes of genital stimulation isn't the climax of intimacy.

This is my hope for a RELATIONSHIP that exemplifies commitment and is the desire of other couples. Our RELATIONSHIP should be about communication the prerequisite to understanding, our RELATIONSHIP should be about trust the foundation of loyalty, our RELATIONSHIP should be about passion the pathway to ecstasy, our RELATIONSHIP must be rooted in LOVE the beginning and the end.

Our LOVE will be the testimonial of unity begotten by JOY, PAIN, STRUGGLE, SUCCESS, FAILURE, TRIUMPH, POVERTY, WEALTH, FAILURE, SUCCESS, LOVE, ANGER, DOUBT, AND FAITH.

Therefore, I invest my soul, my spirit into our RELATIONSHIP and I PRAY.

Valentine's Day

Cupid is a bastard baby, what he know about love, still peeing in bed. Red hearts, roses and violets, and chocolate kisses for a day. What is a Valentine? People asking each other, Baby be my Valentine? Acting warm and fussy for one day. He lying, she crying many days leading up to February 14th, lover's day jubilee!

Just another day the propaganda pimps seduce the public, bank account terrorist, steadily plotting to invade people's wallets. This day set aside to tell my mate she special. Nonsense, if I don't make her feel special at least one day a week, she needs another lover and I need an arrow shot in my ass by a baby with a smelly pamper, Cupid.

But nonetheless,
HAPPY VALENTINE'S DAY!

She Gone, She Flew Away

You know Jackson 5 song "I want you back"?
That's how I feel ya'll,
Wish I could have one more chance

A giving heart, a strong sister, my dream ya dig.
Me, not fully mature, I didn't appreciate her,
Selfish, I let her go as you would a captured bird.
LET IT GO, IF IT COMES BACK, IT WAS MEANT TO BE.
I'm wishing it were true
Because I want her back.

She gone, She flew away,
I didn't invest in the commitment as she did.
I didn't cheat, just didn't invest in communicating honestly how I felt.
Now, I am ready to give the Love she wanted,
She Gone, She flew away,
As a captured bird set free, she didn't look back.
I'm watching the sky, returning to all the familiar places,
Hoping to see her, to no avail,
She gone, and I want her back, yeah, yeah baby.
I hear Jackson 5 singing that song "I want you back."
I can't get that melody out my head.

Prose Poetry

Love Supremacy

My heart considers the matter concerning love is it a feeling,
a word?
My maker touched my emotions, I felt loved.
My maker embraced my spirit it felt like a hug.
my maker is love.
Love pursued me for many years,
unfaithful plenty of times
Yet, Love was and is.
My maker, God.
God is Love

Poet and Painter

I'm engulfed in the ideal of this picture man and woman intertwined by spirit and mind.

I've envisioned a story like none other set in present time, urban atmosphere; two characters a poet a painter and their story consist of the pursuit of passion in life and art so he wrote a poem to reveal the picture in his heart concerning the painter.

I'm captivated by the painter's personality and beauty. I envision a life with the two of them together the poet writes the words to the painter's visionary art,

The painter makes the lyrics of the poet come to life; the expression of divine art is conceived by this organic relationship evolved out of fragile beginnings.

The painter inconsistent, yet stable, the poet unstable yet firm they are searching for the same footprints on a path to truth and self-discovery.

Their hopes are similar, they dream to be healthy and complete. They desire to produce art inflamed with passion that inspires the masses who struggle with common existence versus divine purpose.

Unicorn in Sahara

In a dream that vanishes
However, you remember the images
Love to sleep again just for the pleasure
Of having the dream again
Time passes, haven't dreamed in a while
Slowly forget the images,
It disappears as a dream

Like a unicorn, unique beauty
I saw her then,
She was gone,
I didn't forget her appearance
Her Beauty,
Leaves a permanent impression.
Like a dream you want to remember

She's like the Sahara,
Sun makes her brown skin shine like crystals in sand
She was an angel sitting on clouds
A view of heaven after day,
But just before night

The One

I need one woman to explore this garden of life
We can plant and harvest as one.
She embodies the Essence of femininity, divinely created,
she is vivacious.
My manhood is enhanced by our companionship
One woman who'll be my Inspiration
My woman, my sight if blindness should overcome me
My woman, my cheerleader if despair should challenge me
I need One Woman
To create a garden of life,
With Me.

What can I do with U?

Ca-sa-ra-sara, Aku-na-ma-tada, whatever
This here, how I feel, what I want
I want to know why Stevie wrote My CHERIE amore
Twenty-five years from now wake up with you
Inhale and exhale
Tell you I still adore U
Hoping for U to be more than a friend,
I hope you'll, be my candy girl, now & later
Wanna know U completely, maybe you my soulsista
Help me grow, culminate me,
Absorb your, soul, and body
Understanding you, learning how to love U
Comprehend your spirit.
I see a woman, sassy, and classic
Here's the answer to your question what should you do with me
Separate Steve from the rest of the men, knocking on your door
Give me an opportunity to know U,
Be your companion, comrade, comforter, and caregiver
Be your soul mate, savior, security and support
That's what U can do with Steve.

Frustrated Artist

Full of ambition, dreams, ideas and visions
How to succeed at my craft is a mystery
I am talented and full of expression
What should I do?
Where should I go?
Who is my link?
Why haven't I manifested yet?
I wanna release my joy, pain, triumph, failures
Passions, of my heart and mind
Right now, I'm trapped in a cage flustered as a bird
Who has wings but can't fly
For now, constipated imagination, millions of ideas trapped in
subconscious reservoirs
Thirsty for water and a saline solution
Any solution!
That will allow my emotions to release
so I can be free
Just a relief,
for me,
Frustrated Artist

Thinking About Music

I want to be supreme like the tone of the saxophone
Easy like Sunday Morning, as Lionel Ritchie
Laid back with my honey on my mind in a lounge chair
On the beach in Barbados
Relaxing with a fruit smoothie sensation
Strawberries, melon, guava, and banana
Mixed together in crushed ice
Freezing my teeth, tongue, and brain
I want to be High from 16 bars from
Common, BlackThought & BlackStar
They spit ill-legal lyrics with metaphors and similes
Compare and contrast like Checkers and Chess
You know that authentisizm from within
Like it was free styled in spiritual dimensions before phonic
Yeah I want to feel High
Euphoria and Ecstasy without a drug
Enjoying the art of music
Escape to Barbados.
But damn!
I'm just free styling with my saxophone,
Listening to Hip Hop
On a Sunday by the pool with a virgin daiquiri,
Thinking about Music

Untitled

Blow off steam, lift weights, run miles, or take a trip.
Many choices.
I choose? (Pause)
Work a 9-5, hustle dope, or rob a bank
Create some beats or hang in the streets
Just do me.
Which is? (Pause)
War, Religion, Revolution
Lost in a masquerade,
Don't worry, be happy!
Mercy, Mercy Me or Inner-city Blues
But Everything is Everything,
And Nas said, "I can."
What now? (Pause)
Buy some land
Lease a Lexus
Find love
OK! (Pause)
Seek wisdom
Find truth
Get understanding
Now! (Pause)
I'll wipe myself
Flush the toilet
Wash my hands
And Live.

Mixed Drink

See my faith has been shaken and stirred like a dry martini.
Hope diluted as cognac overwhelmed by ice cubes.
Deceived by my heart, like 90% cranberry, 5% gin,
Facts blended with lies, fear, doubt, and honesty,
sort of strawberry daiquiri.
Bartender can I have a mixed drink?

Ummm, how about some dumb and dumber,
I mean rum and coke or foolishness and wisdom.
Second thought, wine will be fine, merlot and whiskey.
What?
I mean madness with kindness.

Finally, after trying so many mixed drinks,
I settled on an Absolute.
The Christ Revelation-Holy, pure, 100% proof, no ice, no juice.
I drank it, straight, chest burning with goose bumps.
I have found satisfaction, no mixed drink could compare.

Fist of Fury

Lately I've been thinking about death or dying not that I'm ready to go. I really want to live rather than just existing, so I take the death of others more seriously. Thinking about who they became, what they did while on earth. Asking questions like, did they fulfill their dreams, did they discover their purpose in life? What type of tree did they grow to be, from the seed they once were?

Then I get frustrated and angry about things the children suffer. More like what 2Pac said," They got money for war, but can't feed the poor." People living off the fame of the drug game so the curse continues. Will the child make it to 25 years old, shorty wanna be a thug rapper, being an athlete not first on the list no more.

Do you see the good dying, leaving for paradise why we still here looking at the sign of times. Instead of truth revealed some rather be lied to.

Lil girls getting sexed like crazy, having babies at an alarming rate, stunted growth. They're handicapped at becoming mature women because their hearts callous from having to think like a man yet act like a lady, they aren't suppose to learn life that way, it's like they hunters feeding their young, because a sorry motherfucker left her alone struggling designed for nurturing yet she has to protect and provide too. She yells, "it's hard out here, Imma do what I gotta do!"

So, sometimes I cry as Jeremiah did because, at times I see what God see, feel what God feel, yet my anger makes me want to zap a sucka with a lightning bolt, but Love say no, Grace say wait, Hope say maybe, Faith say believe.

Now I'm thinking about life in the context of death, desiring to experience passion in a passionless society, yet I'm glad I live as an American.

Do you observe What's Going On according to Marvin Gaye, The Sign of the Times according to PRINCE, or is it Me against the World according to 2Pac and will there be Life after Death according to Biggie.

Forgive me I'm just unleashing my frustration with my Fists of Fury like Bruce Lee.

Piece of Pie

You got that whole pie to yourself
I know you recognize me salivating for a piece.
I don't want a large piece just enough to taste the
Peaches, sugar, cinnamon.
So, you continue to tease me looking at the pie then glancing at me,
I want to ask but I shouldn't have to, you don't need the whole pie
to yourself.
It's not healthy for you,
I'm thinking of a plan to get me a piece of pie.
My urge of necessity for dessert has taken over.
It would have been simple if common
sharing as humans was applied.
So, I dove over the table face first hand stretched out as if I'm sliding
for home plate,
My face landed in pie mouth chewing peaches.
My anger wouldn't let me enjoy the flavor
I lifted my head and spit the peaches on the floor.

Ill-shit

Real as they come he was loyal, he lost his mother early in life, reared by older brothers and hoodlums, destined to die early. He dogging bullets and suicide.

Thug by nature the heart of Robin Hood, if enemies infiltrated he'd die for his neighborhood. Skin the color of midnight, stout, a streets disciple.

Prior felony convictions have his hands tied, he wouldn't slang if he didn't have to but he has to survive. He politic the block daily, a streetwise representative, the game is crazy, he live with lead in his mouth from the gunshot, got the mark to prove it, on his left cheek.

He deserves to be mentioned he's a friend of mine, his life is real, and the way he choose to

Live, that's Illshit.

Papa never home lived his life in the streets, 30 something years he invested in the penal system, the other 10 chasing the ghost, every drug been created daddy was its whore.

He did whatever necessary just to get high, just living enough for the city.

Kids still love him but he doesn't appreciate it, he'd deceive and manipulate them just to get crack. He don't care just wanna escape, God won't let him leave, no early release date for him, he owe child support, and not monetary.

Priceless experiences, a student of Hard Time, put him in a cell, he produce ill rhymes, a poetic dopefeind with an ill mind. He deserved to be mention he's a relative of mine,

His life is real, and the way he choose to

Live, that's Illshit.

Father Story

I thought I should write this piece
So much going through my head
Can't sleep

Anger

Is what I feel when I think of you
Some of the things I have gone through,
I won't blame, I am a grown man too.
Why you leave me to figure this out on my own
No support, no discipline, no encouragement
Nothing from you to make me strong
Therefore, I have to pretend I am a man, because I am

Disappointed

I watch them they come from two parent homes
Two incomes, two cars, two voices of guidance
Not all the homes were successful, but they tried
Did you even try? Sorry you had no guidance

Mercy

I have to be merciful to you because
The same thing I experience you experienced too,
No direction, no support, no knowledge
Unfortunate,
Wish a Good Father raised you

The Cell

Small, narrow length and width size of four portal-potties
Two beds, two toothbrushes, two windows, two lights, two lockboxes
One toilet, one sink, and one door with a window.
This cell is a bedroom, living room, bathroom, and kitchen
The Cell.
It's an efficiency suite cost taxes payers $40,000.
The Cell
Clean white walls, a polished floor you can eat off.
I thought this cell would be different
From the county jail.
I was wrong,
A cell is a cell.

P.S.

Today, I comprehend mercy; many people don't have anyone to depend on. People make mistakes and fail often. It's challenging to change a behavior or reverse cellular cycles of life.

I observe people, who've committed offenses. Various attitudes with personalities that influence circumstances. Prison, is it rehabilitation or punishment to correct behavior? Neither works!

Lock Up

6a.m. lights come on, door still locked.
Get up brush my teeth
Chow time, swallow the slop
Lock Up.
Breakdown recipe: corn chips, Velveeta cheese, Rumen noodles,
  tuna, baby shrimp, pickles, mayo, honey, onions, mushrooms,
  potatoes (high cholesterol diet)
Lock Up.
Recreation: dips, push ups, sit ups, chin ups,
Crunches, basketball, volleyball, and fights.
Lock Up.
Conversation: judicial case, sentencing, snitches, bitches, cars,
  money, block politics, guns, dope, sports, prison news.
Lock Up.
Lifestyle: thugs, criminals, and misinformed fuckups guilty or innocent,
Locked Up,

Goodies

Different ingredients all compounded together to become tasteful delights. Everyone wants and needs goodies to survive in the county jail. Goodies take the form of money, stocks, bonds, and commodities. He that possess Goodies is profitable. Make a deal or steal, people need some Goodies. Friend may become foe, even for Goodies, They are inexpensive yet possess much value, like batteries for your flashlight on a journey through a dark cave. Goodies can be sweet or salty; expedient but harmful; tasty yet unsatisfying.

Boots

Black leather up to my shin, attention to detail,
teamwork is the key.
Discipline and order are the lessons learned.
Control and authority shape the attitude.
Brotherhood is the honor code that keeps you alive.
Black Boots marching two by two at the
command of the Drill Sergeant.

Brown suede up to my ankles, do what you're told
keep your mouth shut.
Correction, reform, and institutionalization the process endured.
Confinement and submission modified behavior.
Inmate is the status of the new existence that explains this bondage.
Brown Boots walking in parallel lines to chow at the
observation of the Correction Officer.

Various Boots I've worn, some for style others by force
Yet for whatever reason it was my choice.
Boots on my feet for cushion on this rugged journey
Every pair of Boots I've worn tells a story.

Soldier's Pressure

He's a soldier but the war getting the best of him.
Why he do it?
Son had a future nobody saw his pain.
Why he do it?
Did he know someone could help him?
Why he do it?
Leave his family to suffer the pain of losing him.
Why he do it?
A beautiful gift that only happens once.
Why he do it?
Now his children fatherless, so many questions.
Why he do it?
Stop fighting, stop believing, and stop dreaming.
Why he do it?
Did anyone see him struggling or witness his pain?
Why he do it?
Become a victim to his own demise.

Victim's Plea

Before I die, I want you to know somebody loves me and we both will be affected by this tragedy.
I'm the child of a mother, father, I'm someone's brother, sister, I'm the reason for someone else's existence but u about to kill me
U have no legitimate reason.
So, before I die I want u to know I was born with a purpose and my dreams are still valid yet unfulfilled,
I hope for better days for all humanity, I sing songs of love and liberation,
I imagined I'd die in my sleep but u're here to murder me
It's not my time to go
But, before I die remember u will never forget me
I'll haunt u in u're sleep and speak to u when u don't want to hear my voice,
I'll live with you,
fool!
And u here to get rid of me isn't life cruel to us both?
By the way, u someone's child,
The reason another lives, yet u're here to kill me
Lastly, before I die let me pray for mercy on both of us,
Let me call my parents, let me eat my favorite feast,
Let me see a flower, let me hear a poem,
Let me smell, let me breathe.
(Inhale/exhale)

Passion

Everyone needs it
Or should know of this
It's the core of life,

The engine inside of Desire.

I've witnessed many people use it
John Coltrane with his Saxophone,
Michael Jordan playing basketball,
Evander Holifield fighting for Championship Belts

The engine inside of Desire.

Passion People!
That is it!

Passion for people!
It is the engine inside of Desire,

Passion let's find it
People!

Poem

Stay Focused!

I Try!
I Fail.
I Tried Again.
I Failed Again.

I Still Try.

Quit Never!
Never Quit!
Focused Still!
Still Focused!

Don't Give Up

Hard Times, I can see, don't need binoculars,
Pockets full of crumbs,
Heart pumping, barely
Anticipation of harder days to come

Don't give up!

Bills! Gas & electric, phone, rent, plus car note,
Stars on T.V. have it all
Next month it starts all over again,
Bills! Gas & electric, phone, rent, plus car insurance

Don't give up!

You see Muhammad Ali fight George Foreman in the Thrilla in Manila?
You see Lance Armstrong race in Tour de France?
You see Magic Johnson excel in his Business?

Don't give up!

Have you seen a homeless person lately?
Have you seen a stray cat?
Have you noticed anything good?

Don't give up!

As for me,
I've failed repeatedly
I have doubts, fears, plus
Bills! Gas & electric, phone, rent, plus car maintenance

However, I have seen my tomorrow
So I fight like Ali, I race like Armstrong, I execute like Magic
My message to you,

Please! Don't Give Up!

Najee's Story (Part 9)

Exams, Essays, Espresso,
I have a lot to do
Not enough time in a day
I wanna relax, Fuck it!

PRESSURE!

Drama, Dreams, Drugs
I have too much on my mind
Need money for books, bills, baby, and lady
What ima do? To hell wit it!

PRESSURE!

Have to go to court,
Shit!
Facing prison time
Judge, sentenced me
Damn!

PRESSURE!

Had my exam pass/fail, whatever,
Felony conviction, drug addiction, and life's affliction,
Focus diminished, hope deferred,
Whatever, Fuck it, Hell wit it, damn!

PRESSURE!

Oh! Brother Hold On! (Letter to Najee)

Yeah! It's hard right now, but be strong
That's your reflection in the mirror.
U made that decision got sent up the river.
Yeah! Its lonely, people phony
And doing a bid is hard without money.
Spirit locked up, dreams on hold,
Frustrated from uncertainty, heart turn cold.

Oh Brother Hold On!

Working 8 hours a day for less than .50 cents an hour
Can't get no privacy not even in the shower
Roadblocks on path
Praying asking God how long will this trial last?
Wanna see better days and have dreams come true
The more you pray, greater the hardship u go through
And u close to the edge. But don't dare jump.

Oh Brother Hold On!

Tuition due and cost steady increasing
Get an education the world keep screaming
Student loans won't be easy to pay
I'm ready to quit, Economy crashing anyway.

Stephen E. Hooks

Oh Brother Hold On!

Sometimes, I go to the edge of the cliff
I've thought about jumping, I experienced the same shit
Yesterday, I was you,
Someone sent me a letter too

So, BROTHER HOLD ON!
BECAUSE CHANGE GONE COME,
IT HAS TO!
Oh BROTHER HOLD ON!
WITH ME.

Najee's Story (Part II)

What can make a young man want to die?
They say what make you laugh can also make u cry.
Unwilling to fight, His future full of hope,
He suffered from the lynching of his rope.
World weighed too much for his shoulders,
To much witnessing of hearts of men becoming colder
Hard to understand his pain, when I have my own.
I suppose he didn't believe when I told him to hold on
Was his pain so unbearable?
What in his mind would make him do something so terrible?
What can make a young man want to die?
PRESSURE.

Ghetto Dreamers

I asked this kid
What is your Dream?
He said, "Love many women and make a lot of cream,
I wanna live like a rapper, athlete, or thug."
I asked, why you want to live like a rapper?"
He said, "Because they have plenty women, nice cars and platinum."
I asked, why you want to live like an athlete?"
He said "Because all the groupies want them, and they have fame."
I asked why you want to live like a thug?"
He said, "Because they have plenty bitches, and make up rules as
they go."
I thought about his dream and questioned
Why so many kids have the same dream?
I came to the realization
Boys think money, toys, and girls
Is everything.

Dream Chasing

There u are again, within my sight, close yet so far
Been following u for years, lost your trail
U always return,
Always, when I need u most
Give me strength and courage to continue.

Tired of hide and seek, touch and tag, Exhausted
Patiently I tarry for u
U hold my desire
But I need a break, a moment to rest.

There u go again, stop teasing me, close yet so far
I'll be half dead when I reach u but the chase is worth it
Keep me stimulated at night; arise early to pursue u
This amazing chase

My Fair Ladies

All three of their names start with the letter D
I loved them all and kept them close to me
Everyday I thought about them constantly
I watched the clock; I gave them equal time

Desire made me wait she kept me wanting more.
Dream opened my heart, she's the one I longed for.
Destiny came near the end she made everything complete.
I love them all; I keep them close to me.

Rush Hours

I do everything in a hurry these days
I work in a hurry
I sleep in a hurry
I eat in a hurry

I hustle!
Multitasking
cook, clean, surf the net,
It's a cycle, I only stopped to write

I write in a hurry
I read in a hurry
I study in a hurry

I hustle!
Thinking
Bills, economy, politics
It's a system, I only stopped to write.

I talk in a hurry
I listen in a hurry
I shit in a hurry
I fuck in a hurry

I hustle!
Hoping tomorrow
I won't be in a hurry,
Tomorrow I will relax,
Tomorrow came and went, because
I hurried through tomorrow,
TODAY.

Saxyphone

Speak with that sexy voice
Vibrate my eardrum in modest tone
Your style curvy, even your straight frame
You make me rise
Pitch high and low,
The smoothness of your flow
Put my mind at ease
Relaxed when I'm with you
I transcend to a higher climax
Pretty young thing,
Make me believe in love
My heart has met desire,
Cupid hit the target
I'm satisfied with you
Simply insatiable,
I want to romance
Day and night never leaving.
I hold you in my arms
Make melodies of delight
We kiss then,
Four play or six play.
When I can't finish the set
Constantly fantasizing
What we'll create next.

$\mathcal{U}$

I don't know much about U
Attracted the first time I saw U
Walk through my imagination U
stimulate my mind I
longed for the opportunity U
Engaged me with your words I
Ask myself what's my attraction 2 U
more than external beauty I
am amazed with the artist in U
Rude sophistication, U
Banana skin complexion, long black feathery hair, petite body I
adore, small feet, small waist, pointy hips, narrow thighs, I
Gaze with Brown eyes at pear size paps I
Imagine the rest I
am curious why U interest me, I
enjoy conversations U and I
But, U and I
Might have potential
I desire to know U

Untitled

Searching as a raider pursuing an ark
Looking in the bosom of strangers
Listen to music oldies and new
I need it!
Sleepless like a child on Christmas Eve
Frustrated and fatigue
Gazing at the ceiling yet imagining life on Mars
Poetry!

It's here, there, everywhere
On the corner were the miscreants gather
Movie when loving couple shares popcorn
The souls of humanity whether sorrow or laughing
In music, hip-hop, R&B, country, and gospel
But, most of all
Jazz!

I smell it at favorite restaurant
I touch it with my family, friends, and enemies
I taste it on thanksgiving
I desire it more than sex
I hope this feeling will last forever
Love!

I hear u John
(Love Supreme)

I hear it in the horn
I think I have
Words for a song

I know God loves me—why?
Nighttime after the show
I wanna get high.
Explored the neverland of tomorrow
Forgetting my yesterdays of sorrow

Blue Magic be calling even on stage

Resist for the moment
Passion for my horn
Sets me free
Commune with my higher self
Through this saxophone
From birth to death
From hell to heaven
Descend and ascend
Through the saxophone

Blow out joy and pain
Hate Jim Crow
Prejudice white people
On the front row
Hear my horn
But don't see me.

My wife, I love
But this addiction
It's in my blood

Blue Magic in my veins

I love my horn
It's keeping me alive
My favorite thing
My ascension
My afro blues
My spiritual
My funeral too
A Love Supreme, a love supreme, a love supreme . . . .

Beautiful Night

A beautiful night
the wind walked gently by
Earth smelled fresh as clean linen
I sat still and watched, I sat still and listened
I heard the night speak to me,
A beautiful voice
I admired the night we shared quality time
Beautiful night, I thanked God
I'm alive this night
I took a picture with my mind
Hope always to remember this beautiful sight
Beautiful night, I thanked God
The stars shined like illumine crystals
Beautiful night, I thanked God
I write tonight to remember
Beautiful night.

I wish

Upon my night watch
I wished we were never here
I wished everyone was the same color
I wished drugs didn't exist
I wished guns didn't exist
I wished poverty didn't exist
I wished crime didn't exist
I wished ignorance didn't exist
I wished war didn't exist
I wish until there was nothing more to wish for
I awoke and none of my wishes were granted.

Will U Be Mine?

My heart hasn't changed
U my desire
But u know how love
Can be fire and ice
This is real

Get my plans together and marry u
Connected like Hedcliff and Claire Huxtable
Cause I've seen essence untouchable
Then we'll flow to places
Only lovers go
View of sunrise mornings
And constellation party nights
Poetic by design

But the question on my mind
Will u be mine?

I believe the time is now
Let's not wait any longer
Wanting u for awhile
Desire keeps getting stronger
Don't procrastinate
No more excuses
Question in mind
Will u be mine?

Happy Valentine's Day

With Me? Listen!

Self defense mechanism activated
Male rejection repellant smell
Blasting from your body
But
Listen!

With me U don't worry about getting played
Game is out of my league
With me essence of life is of value
With me intimacy surpasses sex
With me peace is a priority
With me your desires are important
With me I see U smiling
With me patience is practiced
With me honesty is honorable
With me compromise is reasonable
With me I believe we can evolve
With me traveling is therapeutic
With me your art is appreciated
With me your ideas are important
With me u can be a liberated woman
We become a better US

One Love

Grandma's Love
The backbone of my family tree
Showed me how to be strong
Endure pain and keep moving on
                    Plus

Mother's Love
Reason I'm here today
Nurtured and encouraged me
Everyday praying, God's grace keeping me safe
                    Plus

Sister's Love
Concerned for me as if I'm her son
Always there when I need her
A gift from God, a special one
                    Plus

Friend's Love
Appreciate me for being me
Allow time for growth
Understanding the blessing of being free
                    Plus

Godfather's Love
Showed me how to be a man
Responsible and faithful
Take care of family pray as often as u can
                              Equals
God's Love
Ultimate satisfaction
Universal and supreme
Sum everybody together
Outcome is
One Love

Poem

4 Grandma Sara

Angels

Could it be the elder lady sat on the porch?
Watching us play
Asking for mercy on us, under her breathe she pray.
Maybe my teacher who made me behave in class
Told me that I'm a genius so don't act like an ass
My friend that kept me strong while I did prison time
Sent me letters and postcards with words that relieved my mind

Stressing these problems getting the best of me
Why can't I find opportunity?
Ma called said she still believe in me
Don't quit Son fulfill your destiny
Time running out and what does the future hold
Before long, I'll be thirty years old
Depressed and singing the blues
Then I remember Grandma Words,
Other people have it worst than you.

New month and bills are due
The pressures of life may overwhelm you
Day is going sour; you hide it so no one knows
A child walks past and smiles
Radiant, uncontaminated of guile

Praise for Grandma

A martyr of love
Cook, clean, pray, shop for antiques, hats and
Pick through garbage,
Don't throw anything away she say

Grandma—wonder woman

I watched her battled
Cancer disease
And won!

She loving yet stern
Grandma look
Message from her eyes

She was strong yet tender
Survival in her blood, passed down from her ancestors
Battled with cancer three times

She calls in the middle of her fight
Make sure you alright
She bless me still
Her life still shine
I witnessed a miracle in her humanity
A resilient spirit although her body was dying.

Let your life Speak for you!

Lived for seventy-plus years
Made no excuses for the things she did
Life deals everyone its share of cards
Play your hand with wisdom
It shouldn't be hard
I knew this woman
She worked with her hands
Many relied on her milk
Love as warm as a cherished quilt
Grandma left me this jewel from her living
I remember the words still
"Stevie, Let Your Life Speak For You."

Sarah, Sarah, Sarah!

I watched the battle
Didn't know anyone could
Be that strong
Everyday taking pills with prayer
Insulin shots in thigh or stomach
No fear in your eyes

Sarah, Sarah, Sarah!
A champion in my eyes

Cancer didn't destroy you
Fought it to the end
Breast cancer attack was your first war
Couldn't stop you
Came back for more
Lung cancer attack second war
Never smoked a cigarette
Told death to flee
Wasn't ready to go yet

Sarah, Sarah, Sarah!
A hero in my eyes

Now I'm here to soldier on
With memories of U
To keep me strong
I miss the endurance U portrayed
Silent prayers U prayed
Hope in your words
Wanting to leave
Stayed longer
For the family

Chemotherapy stripped U
Of your feminine estrogen
But can't overcome
The beauty of your essence
Eating to fill the void
Deadly medicine—poison infusion
Body overwhelmed with fatigue
Still marched on
Back and forth
To the doctor
My God! U Strong!
Survived the worst
Rarely cried
Never complained
I heard you sang many nights
I hope to be as strong as you

My reward
To witness
The greatest fight
Never shown on television
A fight for life
Unselfishly U Loved
I saw the battle
U won!

February 18 2001
After defeating cancer
U decided to rest
U decided to be done!

Sarah, Sarah, Sarah!
My Grandmother
A hero of mine.

Grandma Sarah

Sat by her grave reminiscing
Departed 6 months ago
God took her soul
Today I miss her deeply
I want to see her eyes
Which gave me strength
Hear her voice wouldn't mind her yelling at me
Smell the fragrance she puts in the air
Her name on the marker
Sarah
A blessing indeed
Sarah is her name
Raised nine trees from her good seed
Sarah
On my mind

Najee's Redemption

For the mother who screams
Can you help my son?
He's dying
Yet he lives
He eats, He sleeps
And walks the earth in a daze

Dear mother don't fret
He shall live again
He shall rise
To become a man
If you see him that way
If you love him
Pray for him
If you believe in him
Affirm his gifts and talents

For the father who is silent
Void of the bond
And ignores his son's voice
Yet he lives
He eats, He sleeps
And walks the earth in vain

Dear father be courageous
You shall live again
You shall rise
And become a savior
If you can love yourself
If you will save your family
If you desire health
If you will listen
The mother scream
She said, "Save our Son."

Papa's pain

Red, blue scars with deep bruises
Unseen with natural eyes
Pain inherited from past generations
Shortage of maternal touch
abandoned at young age
Paternal neglect also
Adolescent void of parental protection
Denied of father's discipline
Miseducated by peers,
Confusion evident
Intelligent, artistic, a street poet and philosopher
But who will listen?
Gifts entrapped in fortified stone, imprisoned
Enslaved by pain unseen with natural eyes
Bleed black blood
Internal toxins
tears escape thru his urine
No empathy for his pain,
No one stretches forth their arms with understanding
Mother gone, Father gone, sister gone, brother incapacitated
Papa alone and pain is his guardian

Don't Cry Man

He Hurting within, raw emotion
Burdened with regret
Crippling his soul

Don't cry man!

I'm tough I'll be all right
Give me more challenges I can fight
More agony more stress
Bring it on, I'll get stronger

Don't cry man!

If tears flow
Retract them back
Made to endure this shit
A man not a wimp

Don't cry man!

Wounded internally
Incapacity to feel
Can't release the pain
Built to be strong
No signs of weakness
Might hurt my name

Don't cry man!
Damn what a shame!

Send Love

You not forgotten
I remember back in the day
YOU—YOUR style
Hustle and flow
Stay true
Love ya for it
Despite these circumstances
In time
I send you love
You on my mind

In case your spirit
Downtrodden and low
I reminisce when
Life was simpler
Adolescent years
Playing ball, and chasing girls

And chores
Yeah!
Those days gone, we never
Anticipated this Ill-Shit
Present today

For my people behind
The walls
Set ya mind free
"Trap the body, but not my mind"
Fortify ya spirit and let ya body follow
Transcend the system
One Love

Last Words

Hope, a word
I build my tomorrow
Faith I hold on to
In my heart
Before I die

But truth
Be told
Don't look like things
Will get better before
I'm old

Money rules the world
People say
Be right, be wrong
We'll all find out on judgment day

Last words spoken from a Man
In search of Life
I hope and believe it
To be better
In my next life.

Papa's Pain

Sing: sitting at the dock of bay watching time roll away
Sitting at the dock of the bay wasting time

See papa pain run deep
Vietnam nights
So the needle helps him sleep
Served in a war
Home life not the same as before
Hard loving his wife and three kids
Heroin head, alcoholic
Living yet dead
I saw him few
He looked good
But smelled stale.

Papa's pain run deep

Sing: sitting here getting high watching my life pass me bye
Sitting here getting high wasting time

See daddy's pain run deep
From his papa's pain
So he can't sleep
No parental guidance
Snatched by the streets
Hustling, stealing, robbing
17 years old state pen
Steady mobbing
Alcohol, heroin, acid, cough syrup, cocaine, crack
Got him
He can't die
He wants to
As if the pain in living isn't enough.

Sing: sitting here stressing my mind watching my time roll away
Sitting here getting high wasting time

My pain was deep
Cause daddy's pain was deep
And I couldn't sleep

Cause I never saw daddy
Home
Never heard him say
Son
So I searched for
One
I looked for daddy
Where he looked
To the streets
There I found some
Like papa, like daddy, like me

Why Ma meet daddy?
She could have done much better
Was she high?
I know he was
Or doing jail time
Does anyone remember him?
When he wasn't
Messed up, drugged up, fucked up
I wish he were a real man
A hero but instead
He gave up living
Settled being a zero
Damn!
Why won't he fight and win
Rather than wait to die

Whistle out: sitting here bye the dock of the bay . . .

Prison Poems

Poems/Writings from Steve (Dad)

"Steve the sharing of my poetry is all that I have, and I pray that you discover the me that everybody don't see!"

Words from one of the letters Steve (Dad) wrote while in prison.

Dad and I began to develop a relationship around 1995-1996, He was in prison and I was transitioning from my experiences in street life. We began exchanging letters. I was searching for answers to my life.

Dad wrote beautiful poems during his prison stays. He sent me many of his writings over many years. I'm not a pack rat so overtime I threw them away or misplaced them.

During that time I got to know Dad, every time he was incarcerated I'd learn a little bit more about him. Crazy, I know, but I spend the time I longed for as a boy with Dad when he is locked up and sends me letters.

When he comes home from prison his lifestyle reverts back to what got him sent to prison in the first place. I know where to find him if I want to see him, but I get tired of looking for him. Unfortunately, the only time I truly find him is when he's at home in some prison cell, when he's sober and free to explore his soul. I want to know my dad, I'd rather him locked up so I can receive his writings, in which I discover him that nobody else see.

"Maybe"

Had I been a super-star, millionaire
Or even a good father
Who had taken us somewhere?

Maybe

Had I not been a product of my environment
Drug-addicted
And dead-beat Dad

Maybe

If I could have understood
How important, my offspring would be
I could be the poet
That God gifted me to be

Maybe

Just maybe
You would understand
How very very
Much yo Daddy needs & love
You so much

Maybe!

Your Dad

Written for
Stevie 11-5-06

Three Hundred & Sixty degrees of Man According to Pop

Steve this poem is from me to you!

Three hundred sixty degree
Is a full circle
The father, son+ Holy Ghost
Is three hundred Sixty degree!
Man was made and created by God
In the full circle that God blew
Woman was created from man by God's
Hand he removed one of mans ribs
With the breath of life he blew,
Peace, love, Knowledge, understanding + responsibility
Three hundred sixty degrees
Make a man.
Winter, spring, summer and fall
Apart of
Three hundred sixty degree
Of a man!

Written for: Stevie
Composed By: Steve j. Hooks
1-10-07

"It Aint YOU"

Dear you, guess who?
It's the me that you always see
But never listen
Sometimes I see me
But I cannot
Recognize who I am
At other Times I recognize
But don't realize
That it's me!
When I try to introduce me
To myself, I always wind-up acting like
Someone else
Fifty-two years
Me +you have been together,
The good and the bad times;
I know me but at times,
I don't understand you
I've asked others

Stephen E. Hooks

What should I do?
Some say
You're good people
And it's me who
Thinks that I'm all that,
But those
Are the one's listen to you
Because they don't see me.
So I talk to myself
Because there's no one to talk to
"But me"
And the me I see, aint you . . .

Written by: Steven J. Hooks

"No More Yesterdays"

I woke-up this morning and it was still
Yesterday and everywhere,
I'd go the pain
Just wouldn't go away/ every corner
I turned things kept on being the same
I begged, borrowed+ stole,
Yet I couldn't get
Away from yesterday/ I met "today", dreamed
Of tomorrow, still I couldn't get away from
Yesterday!
I went to prison over + over trying to get
Away from my yesterdays
Only to discover
My today was still yesterday.
So I got down on my knees asked God
To please please take me away from yesterday
And when I got up it was today
And if it were His will
I'll see a tomorrow and my yesterday
Will all be gone away!

Written by: Steve James Hooks

For: Steve, Sherina+Grandson's

Along the Way

I was blessed early in life with two of two
Two man-child+ two woman, who never
Were children for little girls are born grown.
I never played with toys grand pop said
That the twenty-two rifle was not a toy, it was
For hunting food, but the first thing shot was a
Nigga! From the boy's club to the rec yard;

Along the Way

The first 36 months from 19-23, I swore
To God I knew what to do back in the game after
Doing three the hard way I lasted 8 funky months
And fell on my face again, for twenty six more
Months, This a way thata way I ran "fuck parole
I said" so I jumped and ran, my Grandma who
Was my pride+joy God had called for her, while
I was doing time

Along the Way

Mama told me about days like this yea payen
For the things, that I got away with is what got me
In this mess, now don't get me wrong
Many tears have I shed and many of days
I should have been dead!
I came up I fell down I made babies I
Loved I hated I pimped and I tricked.

Along the way

Written By: Mr. Steven J. Hooks

Untitled

Couple of weeks ago, Sherina and I talk
Every blue moon. Parris and I talk
Almost everyday. Steve came to my
House last week we chilled out for a
While. I love you Daddy. 4Real. I don't
Hate you, I just disagree on your
Decisions in life that's all. I always
Wish that we had a better
Relationship. My mother never really
Talked about you to me growing up
Sometimes I would ask questions and
She wouldn't really say much or just
Didn't respond at all. My point is I
Really, feel like I don't know you.
When my big brother come to my
House last week, we were talking
Then he handed me a piece of paper
With your name on it. For a second I
Wondered why he even gave it to me,
Like I felt like I could care less about
Talking to you like you were
Pointless to my vision. I don't like
Treating dirt for dirt or holding
Bad memories. Daddy the life that you
Do its hard out here sometimes I know,
And I'm not talking down on you or
Anything like that I'm saying life
Is short and I don't wanna lose you so soon.

For my sister Teair, Sorry T!

Sparkling Twenty-99

Within those Sparkling brown eyes
I see the love of a million times
The love of your mother+me from
The seed that God gave me!
Your Beauty, Sparkles at Twenty-II
And will shine at twenty-nine
But please, always stay true to everything
Your mother taught you for it's nice to
Be important but it's far more important
To be nice!
My Sparkling Twenty II yo daddy will
Always love you, and anytime you don't
Understand take yo worry to God for he
Has our plans!
Just because you're Twenty II. There's no
Star brighter for me then you!

You're a birthday everyday that you live
So be Happy and share the love, that
God so graciously gives . . . .

Written by: Dad

Composed for: Ms. Teair Jacquelyn Dawson

For Lyrik (My niece) LA LA BY

I said hush little baby don't
You cry grand-pa going to tell
You about some la la by, sometimes
La la bys won't sing but when
You get older, "I'll get you a golden
Ring.
Now when times get hard and your
Ring don't shine, think about grand-pa
And you'll smile every-time
Every now + then your smile may
Fade then you can see how
Wonderful you were made!
Make your mama remember grand-pa
Because he loves you too!

Written by Grand PA
Mr. Steven J. Hooks

"If I Knew"

Playen the street life where
Everything is fair, except watching
Your youth go by while you
Stare!

If I Knew

Finger popen, layen, playen
And pimpen is in the air
Then maken babies like you
Just don't care

If I knew

Time after time, prison after
Prison, I dreamed of being true
Yea stayen true to the game
And coming up like ah playa
I suppose to do

If I knew

They say how can you play by the golden rule in a crowd
That doesn't play fair

If I knew

Taxes, death, and trouble are
Three things that for sure
And if you walk with a
Lame you surely will come up
With a limp

If I knew!

Now I know that being Lame
Is really, what's hip, instead of
Layen, playen and pimpen and
Comen up with a limp

If I knew

So take if from ah playa who
Came up lame in and out of
Prison is not really a game

If I knew

Poetry is a gift being able to
Draw a picture with words
Telling life story's of the games
People play and more

If I knew

Nothing is new under the sun
Regardless of what they say
Or how we try to run

If I Knew

Being the rich man that God
Made me and the ungrateful
Slave that I am I rebuke my
Yesterdays and embrace the
Morning sun because I never had
To run

If I Knew

Written by:
Mr. Steve Hooks

The Big Picture

Written words that will describe a picture
Of a conflict that continuously goes on within
After thirty-three yrs of self + society imprisonment
I bid good-by to my yesterday while I fight to
Understand my todays!
The wisdom of the moment assures me that
Only if I believe, I can truly walk
Upon water.
Big I's and little U's will forever keep
Your blessings at a minimum, for I
Want for my brother what I want for
Myself it's what will set me free!
To be able to believe in something unseen;
And have trust in the faith. That is true!
I've been lip-locked, brain dead and sold-out
To the forces that be, for far too long.
This foolish pride, even though I'm still
Alive, kept me for the picture that I refuse
To see.
The me that nobody can see, is
Truly you The blessing + the gift of my
Seed that God has finally allowed me to
See!

Written by: Mr. Steven J. Hooks
For: Mr. Stephen E. Hooks

"I am that Nigga"

You know me, you've always known me. I am
That nigger you have hunted and feared night+day:
I am that nigger you have killed hundreds of my
People in a vain hope of finding;
I am that nigger
That in no longer just hunted robbed + murdered.
I am that nigger that hunts you now.
Yes you
Know me!
I am that Nigga

Written by: Saddi Jwanza Nyuhma

This is Dad's Muslim name given him during early 80's prison stay

Peace of Mind

Once again, I find myself waiting
My freedom of tomorrow, even though
I am as free as I'll ever be today!
For freedom being but a temporary
State of mind, when one truly
Understands the here + now.
I've beaten the path of broken
Hearts + wounded spirits, that
Touched my skin+ stole my soul!
Midnight walks thru everlasting
Time, when all I wanted was
A bottle of wine; of the dog that
Bit me or the woman whom left
Me the child who cheered only to
Be imprisoned by the one whom
Wouldn't love me!
So, I'll tip my hat to a little of this or
A little of that knowing that a
Peace of mind is all I've got!

Written By:
Mr. Steve J. Hooks

The Me I Don't See!

As I entertain myself with words of pure
Thought +wisdom, I began to recognize
The me that no one ever sees. The silent
People within myself whom I hardly
Ever talk with, yet I am always listening
To!
One slays the beast another plays the players
While trying to understand the other
Personalities whom also live within
Rent-free is not allowed within the premises
Of my mind especially while I am doing
Time.
While tip towing thru my own mind
I often come across an abundance of people whom never cease to
amaze me but can I
Will surface at any given time!
Writing being my only real reality, I often
Suffer when I repeat the same fantasy realizing
That it's only the here+ now that matters!
Diligently I crown myself for being aware of
All the people within me setting them free from
The cruel fact, that all of them are me!

Written By: Steve J. Hooks

Psalms/ Proverbs

I'm so close to Life It's scary because all this time,
     I thought I was alive.

If you believe that, it's the person next to you, who smells,
     First, smell yourself before you tell the other person they smell.

It's easy to notice what others are doing
     Actually, it's a personal reflection of you so look closely.

To seek and find God is life;
     Live with compassion and mercy on a daily basis is peace.

Give what is available and receive with gratitude.

My friend betrayed me
I wanted to harm him, and then I looked at the harm I caused other
people.
I learned forgiveness.

If you recognize an issue in your friend
     Before judging, look within.

I paid the price of a fool
     I learned wisdom afterward.

Wisdom is the ultimate insurance policy.

Anger and impatience are worst than a tsunami on a bad day.

Protect your name it's worth more than temporary vanity.

Watch your thoughts they will produce a result.

Humility is more powerful than arrogance of the ego
      Although humility will not defend itself.

When adversity came the first time, I was afraid
  I was unprepared, when adversity came the second time
I suffered loss because I was unprepared,
  When adversity came the third time, I said thank you
adversity for coming back.
If you want to change your circumstances,
  Change your perspective
If you want to change your environment, transform your soul.
I sought for success only to discover anxiety,
  I learned to be patient I discovered success.
The rich man is powerless if his name is disgraced.
  The poor man is powerful as long as he upholds his integrity.
The truth is simple to understand
  The arrogant mind makes it complicated.
A man's appetite can be as dangerous as a poisonous snake
  The venom like the appetite will cause harm
It doesn't matter how much you read a religious book
  Do you practice the principles of what you read?
Not until I began practicing what I believe
  Did I find my truth?
I sowed a seed in heaven
  Yet I reaped a harvest on earth
Today I live in gratitude
  Tomorrow I hope to live
When adversity comes do not run
  Stand still and watch adversity's reaction
When I transformed into a man
  The boy within me submitted

My heart got what it wanted
But afterward I was unsatisfied

God show me how to pray again
God lead me to your way again
God forgive me I've strayed again
God my heart has deceived me again
God here I am again
A wise man said, "Never say what you don't have,"
   I say," It's hard to be OPTIMISTIC when you face
   mountains that seem insurmountable.
But
What I do have is PEACE
What I do have is FAITH
What I do have is JOY
What I do have is SELF-DETERMINATION
What I do have is DESIRE
What I do have is AMBITION
What I do have is LOVE
Moreover, with these virtues I am confident
   Now the mountain isn't as fierce as before.
Now, the mountain appears as a hill,
   I have climbed plenty of them before.

What am I searching for?
Uncertain

I will search again
In my heart, I will look
At what I believe

I'm stuck in shit
Somebody help me
They looked at me and laughed

If I had known!

If I had known that trouble don't last always
     I would have said THANK YOU trouble
If I had known the value in people
     I would have been more giving
If I had known, I would make so many mistakes
     I would have been more merciful
If I had known my mother's responsibility
     I would have been more obedient
If I had known, the economic recession would come
     I would have began saving money at 10 years old
If I had known, there was no such thing as job security
     I would have followed my passion a long time ago
If I had known how to love myself
     I would have enjoyed my time being single
If I had known, my brother would die after our fight
     I would have never engaged in warfare
If I had known, she was the woman I should have married
     I would have committed myself to our relationship

My Heart Melody

I am, I am Thank-Full
I am, I am Thank-Full
I am, I am, Thank-Full

I am, I am, Grate-Full
I am, I am, Grate-Full

I'm Thank-Full

For your Mercy
I'm Thank-full
I'm Thank-full

For your Kindness
I'm Grateful
I'm Grateful

Repeat . . . .

Repeat . . . .

Repeat . . . .

Some call you God but a name or a word doesn't exist for what I want to call you, better yet should I say awesome? Or should I call you marvelous? Neither word gives enough splendor and glory that is due you Omega I mean Alpha you are more than this and I am overwhelmed that you notice me and give me a mind and desire to commune with you. God of my soul and see calling you God does not seem to do you justice, you are more than God, Master, Lord, King. What more can I say to describe you My Maker, The Beginning, The Ancient of Days, Almighty, my mind is fatigued at the moment trying to give you an identity more worthy than what I've known and heard about you.

Better yet tell me what I should call you Father, Mother. Oh my soul is perplexed with the matter my spirit is hungry for you, The One who breathe life into me in whom I can only trust to be Love. Wow! And that's not enough to describe you either. Magnificent? Be magnified in me regardless, only you can fulfill my desire. Desire! How about I call you . . . . HOLY

God loves me,
Why am I unfaithful?

My heart is wicked as any other man
Although, I hide from myself.

In my attempts to be good
I still didn't measure up to God

I conceived lust. I lost my way,
Had I known my lust for her
Would leave me empty
I would have cut out my eyes

I'm overwhelmed so I write
To release the stress
Instead of masturbate or have
Meaningless sex.

I will not run away from God
I will run towards God
God is
All I have in this world

When I lived among the heathens they treated me like sheep led to
    the slaughter
When I lived among the church-goers I met Saints although most
    Sinners
And the conclusion of the matter People is People.

I took the first step to success
    The first step was faith
I took another step
    But there was no step there.
I have learned a valuable lesson in life
    The principle of Desire and Detachment
To want something or someone with passion
    Then be able to liberate yourself with the same passion

I looked for wealth outside my soul
    I found more poverty
I searched for wealth within my spirit
    I found immeasurable treasures

In the morning, if I awake,
    Heart of mine please be Thankful
It's Grace, Simply Grace.

I've met fear in the alley,
The first time I ran
I met fear again
He had a friend, I ran
I met fear and failure a third time
I walked forward
Stood firm between them,
Until Faith and Courage rose up within me,
Then I walked past fear and failure
Towards my destiny.

They looked in amazement at the man dancing and worshiping his
God
If they only knew his purpose,
They'd stop gazing and join in
Rapture

Wow! God Almighty's

I try to understand Almighty Splendor
        Then Almighty amazes me again.

Though I have weakness as a Man
        I choose to glory as a Divine.

In my weakest moments sometimes I compromise
        But I don't quit fighting to overcome my weaknesses.

Conclusion

I have discovered writing to be part of my salvation. I have learned valuable information about myself through my writing. I don't keep a journal, I write on an as need to basis. My intention in writing is to express myself and become liberated in my mind. I advice you to read Passion and Pain along with Part I my memoir Before I Loved Her I Healed Myself. The non-fiction books are intended to introduce me as an author to my audience. I plan to release my first novel soon after the publication of Passion and Pain and Before I Loved Her I Healed Myself. I noticed most authors write memoirs after they've written many novels; I decided to do the reverse giving my audience more background of my story before reading my stories.

Acknowledgement

Special thanks, to Dave Hershe for financial support. Thank you for being my business mentor. Dave it's divine we met and bizarre at the same time. Jim and Julie Riggs, for empowering me to achieve this. Thanks to my Barbershop family, and Personal Training customers at The Gym at Carew Tower (Cincy) for patronizing my services.

Many thanks to Michael Colbert for creating my book cover. Thank you for taking my words and creating a picture that tells my story. You believed in my passion for creating this work, and gave me your talent free of charge your best. I will repay you with dividends.

Photo Credits

Courtesy Juanita Johnson, Taylormadeimages, LLC

Artistic Credits

Courtesy Michael Colbert, Fine Art Drawing & Painting, mikecolbert@hotmail.com